Out of the Frying pan

into der

BRYAN CHALKER

with additional
photographs by

FELICITY HAZE

REDCLIFFE

Bristol

First published in 1989
by Redcliffe Press Ltd.,
49 Park St., Bristol

ISBN 0 948265 93 0

Typeset by The Picador Group, Bristol
Printed by Penwell Ltd, Callington, Cornwall

CONTENTS

ACKNOWLEDGEMENTS

This book is dedicated to Richard L. Heaume, of the German Occupation Museum, Forest, Guernsey, without whose initial encouragement and continued assistance it would not have been written.

I am also indebted to Peter and Paul Balshaw, of La Valette Underground Military Museum, St. Peter Port, Guernsey, who availed me of their files and exhibits.

Thanks are also due to the following people who provided me with priceless photographs, souvenirs and memories:

Mrs Marjorie Bird; Frank Stroobant; Linda V. Collenette; Mrs A.M. Priddy; J. Elliott; A. & J. Stevens Cox, The Old Curiosity Shop, St Sampsons, Guernsey; Molly Bihet; Tim Wetherall; Jersey Evening Post; Guernsey Evening Press; Channel Television; Peter Girard; K.H. Tough and W.M. Ginns, of the Channel Islands Occupation Society; The Island Fortress Occupation Museum, Jersey; St Peter's Bunker War Museum, Jersey; Joe Mière, of The German Underground Hospital, Jersey.

Of the recipes, Bean & Potato Cake was suggested as a breakfast dish by Dorothy Higgs, Potato Sandwich and Parsnip Pudding were contributed by Marjorie J. Bird, Sweet Corn Pudding and Carrageen Relish by Linda Collenette, Batter in Tomato Sauce and Country Batter Pie by Dorothy Higgs, Tomato Pie by S. G. Pay, Limpet Omelette by J.Elliott, Substitute Junket by V.S.Bryan and Imitation Suet Pudding by K. Le Cheminant.

Thanks, too, to the people of the Channel Islands for making me feel so welcome —and for trusting me.

BRYAN CHALKER

INTRODUCTION

The German Occupation of the Channel Islands has been well documented since their liberation in May, 1945, but little is known on mainland Britain of the remarkable and often heroic efforts of the Islanders to sustain themselves through five years of Nazi rule.

It is easy to forget that the Channel Islands, with their Norman-French way of life, are British and that Britain's war was their war. The Channel Islands were spared most of the devastating bombing inflicted on the mainland by the Luftwaffe, but they experienced the full rigours of war in other ways.

After the declaration of war on September 3, 1939, there followed a lengthy period of inactivity known as the 'Phoney War'. No bombs fell on Britain and threatened poison-gas attacks did not materialize. Small wonder then that the Channel Islands were lulled into a false sense of security. So detached were the Channel Islands from the full reality of war between Britain and Germany that at the beginning of 1940 Jersey published a holiday poster which read: 'The ideal resort for wartime holidays this summer.'

Then came the bombshell. After much deliberation by the Admiralty it was decided that the Channel Islands were untenable and on June 19, 1940, the British Government announced the Islands' demilitarization. It left the Channel Islands in an appalling predicament and evacuation plans were quickly implemented.

Guernsey's population in 1939 was 43,820. It was the most densely populated of the Islands and in 1940 a total of 19,000 people, including children and men of military age, left for England.

German fighter plane refuelling on Guernsey. Note the civilian lorry. (Bundesarchiv Koblenz)

Over 230 Channel Islanders died serving in the British Armed Forces.

Of Jersey's estimated population of 55,000, almost half registered for evacuation but the final number actually to leave for the mainland was reckoned to be about 10,500.

Within ten days of receiving news of the Channel Islands' demilitarization, Hitler acted. At 7.00pm on June 28, 1940, six Luftwaffe Heinkels bombed and machine-gunned the harbour of St Peter Port and outlying areas of Guernsey, killing an estimated thirty people, including the driver of the Guernsey Red Cross Ambulance. Several civilians were reportedly burned to death as fuel escaped from damaged lorries under which they sheltered from the bombing.

St. Helier, Jersey, was attacked at the same time and ten people lost their lives.

Two days later German Occupying Forces landed on Guernsey. Jersey was occupied the next day, with Alderney and Sark yielding to the Swastika on July 2 and 3.

On July 1, 1940, the Commandant of the German Forces in Occupation of Guernsey issued various orders in the local press, including the surrendering of all weapons, the prohibition of motor spirit, the seizure of alcohol, and the assurance that 'The population would be respected but at the least sign of trouble the town would be bombed.' Jersey, of course, received similar orders.

The German authorities stressed repeatedly that 'Life and property of the population would be respected and guaranteed.' Indeed, the first year of the Occupation saw the Germans behaving with restraint and apparently doing their level best to ensure that the civilian population had no undue cause for complaint.

So confident were the Germans of victory over the Allies that one soldier is on record as saying to a Guernsey resident that 'This is only a temporary occupation. You must realise that the war is virtually over.' Few Islanders, or Germans, had any notion that the Occupation would drag on for five long years.

The Occupation soon led to scarce and dreary food and, by the end of 1944, the very real threat of starvation.

Save your **F**ood, Save your Country !

Necessity, though, was the Mother of Invention and, faced with the prospect of a long occupation, deprivation and hunger the Islanders turned their hands to creating weird and wonderful recipes and innovations. They made use of seaweed, potato peelings, limpets, blackberry leaves, sugar beet and seawater – for food, drink, syrup and salt.

White vaseline and refined linseed oil took the place of lard and dripping. Biscuit tins, paper bags, paint pots and milk cans were turned into ingenious cooking devices.

Smokers resorted to puffing lettuce leaves, rose petals, scented burr and clover to supplement their almost non-existent tobacco rations. Conkers, tomato stalks, dried seaweed, gorse, cabbage stumps and tar stood in for coal, coke and wood.

Groups all over Jersey and Guernsey formed themselves into committees, organising communal kitchens and baking facilities to supply the populace. They became a Kitchen Front to be reckoned with: a fighting force of valiant individuals who openly flaunted their continued allegiance to the Union Jack.

As 1944 drew to its dismal close the future looked bleak. Salvation was to come in the form of 'Vega', an antiquated Swedish Red Cross steamship which visited the Islands for the first time on December 27, 1944, with a cargo of medical supplies and food parcels and rescued the population from the brink of starvation.

By a strange twist of fate the Germans suffered a greater degree of hunger than the civilian population. They had no Red Cross food parcels to help them.

HITLER'S ISLAND MADNESS

The German Occupation of the Channel Islands began on Sunday, June 30, 1940. For the first time in nearly 900 years an invading army had set foot on British soil.

The Channel Islands – Jersey, Guernsey, Alderney, Sark and Herm – had been largely independent and self-sufficient for centuries. Situated close to the French mainland the Islands had, nevertheless, remained loyal to the Crown since the reign of William the Conqueror.

The Islands were strategically important to Hitler's war machine and, following their demilitarization – when British military experts declared: 'There need be no fear of the Germans taking any advantage from the British decision to demilitarize the Channel Islands' – the Fuhrer saw his bold but ill-conceived dream of an Atlantic Wall take a further step towards reality. It was also a wonderful opportunity to plant the hated Swastika on British soil and wave it in Churchill's face.

Hitler's concept of a vast Atlantic wall of concrete and steel fortifications was breathtaking. Its deployment of financial resources and human labour was colossal.

The German Chancellor envisaged such a wall guarding the Atlantic Coast from Norway to Spain. It was to be modelled on the 'Siegfried Line', or 'Westwall', and created out of 15,000 concrete defence strongpoints, many of which had been tried, tested and proven during the First World War.

St Peter Port, Guernsey, was earmarked as a U-Boat base.

The Channel Islands – or Den Kanalinseln, as the Germans knew them – were included in Hitler's plan for a coastal fortification network but the deployment of more than 30,000 men spread across Jersey, Guernsey, Alderney and Sark placed too great a strain on the Nazi war machine. Many high-ranking German officers, Rommel included, disagreed with Hitler's obsessive dream of an Atlantikwall and secretly scorned the Fuhrer's Channel Island scheme as 'Island Madness'.

Hitler, of course, would accept no criticism of his masterplan and forged ahead with 'Fortress Channel Islands'. He saw the Channel Islands as the German equivalent of Britain's Gibraltar and Malta defence strongholds.

The enormous numbers of men involved in the construction and defence of 'Fortress Channel Islands' included troops, civilians employed by the Germans, and slave workers of the infamous Organisation Todt. Their task was to construct ferro-concrete and steel fortifications across the length and breadth of the Channel Islands. Alderney was transformed into a huge fortress and concentration camp. Most residents had been evacuated and wartime activity on Alderney was cloaked in secrecy.

Jersey and Guernsey echoed to the thunder of rock blasting and the steady throb of concrete mixers as Hitler's vast building programme got underway. The work included the construction of enormous tunnel complexes, bunkers, gun emplacements, railways, Naval observation towers and battery observation posts.

Such was the extent of the construction programme that by September 1944, a total of 272,000 cubic metres of reinforced concrete had been used in Guernsey and 76,746 mines laid along its coastline and beaches. More than 14,000 tons of rock were removed to build Jersey's 500-bed Underground Hospital. Army engineers laid 67,000 mines around Jersey's coast.

Within a space of four years the Germans had transformed the topography of the Channel Islands forever.

German Naval Observation Tower (MP 4), L'Angle, Torteval, Guernsey.

German Naval Observation Tower (MP 3), Pleinmont, Torteval, Guernsey. Leased by Channel Islands Occupation Society (Guernsey Branch).

Section of Jersey's light railway constructed during the Occupation. (Copyright: Jersey Evening Post)

LIFE GOES ON

To the Channel Islanders, occupation meant more than being overrun by German troops and military vehicles and literally rubbing shoulders with a despised enemy.

Guernsey became the most heavily fortified of all the Channel Islands and at one point it was claimed that there were actually more Germans per square mile in Guernsey than in Germany.

The Occupation brought the immediate collapse of the Channel Islands' economy, which was based on the export of tomatoes and potatoes, and on tourism. In 1939, Guernsey had more than 900 acres of glass-houses in use and exported over 35,000 tons of tomatoes to England.

In addition to its huge exports of potatoes, tomatoes and – to a lesser degree – cream, Jersey derived a generous percentage of its annual income from tourism. Tourism was a well developed industry and in 1940 the island played host to no fewer than 200,000 visitors – incredible figures when one considers that a World War was being waged at the time.

With the arrival of the Germans the Channel Islanders saw their traditional way of life altered over-night. Eagle and swastika replaced Union Jack; driving was changed from the left-hand side of the road to the right. Civilians were issued with German identity cards and labour contracts. British newspapers were forbidden and the Channel Island's press – Jersey's *Evening Post* and *Les Chroniques de Jersey* and the *Evening Press* and *The Star* on Guernsey – came under strict German control. The Germans established their own newspapers in Jersey (*'Deutsche Inzeleitung'*) and Guernsey (*'Deutsche Guernsey Zeitung'*).

Radio transmitters – and later, receivers – were confiscated. Carrier pigeons were outlawed and many killed to provide food for German officers. The Germans later threatened to execute anyone found in possession of a pigeon.

Over five hundred Guernsey families were forced out of their homes to make way for the billeting of German troops; many of the homes were subsequently rendered verminous and uninhabitable. The authorities threatened to shoot anyone found plundering empty houses.

The army requisitioned lorries, cars, motorcycles, bicycles, food, fuel and property and imposed strict curfews and driving bans. On July 22, 1940, clocks were advanced one hour, 'to accord with German time.'

Strangely enough the Germans did not interfere unduly with the Islands' entertainment and most cinemas

Jersey's growing stack of confiscated wireless sets. (Copyright: Jersey Evening Post)

remained open. Between screenings of German propaganda films like 'Dorf Im Roten Sturm' and 'Ich Bin Gleich Wieder Da!' (the latter restricted to viewing by German Forces only), civilians could still watch Preston Foster in 'Chasing Danger'; Warner Baxter and Ceasar Romero outwitting each other in 'The Return Of The Cisco Kid'; and laugh at the gormless antics of George Formby in 'Keep Your Seats, Please'.

Variety shows and musical recitals were staged by local performers. The German authorities were reasonably tolerant of such entertainment but they did take exception to the singing of 'Kiss Me Goodnight, Sergeant-Major', during one concert programme and promptly banned it because, 'it lacked dignity!'

The Germans spent much of their free time during the first few days of Occupation scouring the shops in St Helier and St Peter Port for luxury goods to send home to wives and sweethearts. Stocks of soap, cosmetics, stockings, cameras, razor blades, shoes, clothes and leather goods were quickly exhausted. It was to be more than five years before they were replenished.

To begin with the Germans adopted a subtle 'iron fist in a velvet glove'

German military band marching up the Pollet, St. Peter Port, 1940. (Copyright: German Occupation Museum, Guernsey)

approach in their dealings with Islanders and the population was lulled into a false sense of security. The Gestapo (Geheime Staatspolizei) proper was never truly represented in the Islands.

For a time, it looked as if '. . . their Beethoven and their Bach were really far worse than their bite', as suggested in Noel Coward's wickedly witty song, 'Don't Let's Be Beastly To The Germans'. But the kid-glove approach was nothing more than a clever tactical manoeuvre on the part of the German authorities.

The Islanders had suffered the trauma and pain of losing nearly 30,000 loved ones and friends to evacuation and military service. Red Cross messages published in the local newspapers eventually helped relieve their anguish.

One Guernsey resident, Mrs. Linda Violet Collenette, now in her eighties, remembers the period with great clarity: 'Some of us felt, quite naturally, that Churchill had turned his back on us. We really didn't know what to think. We were British and yet here we were at the mercy of the Nazis. The majority of Germans here in the first few months of the Occupation seemed to be all right. Not at all what we expected. I think some must have been veterans of the Great War, because they were older men and were probably posted here to see the war out. They must have thought they were in for an easy time.

As the Occupation stretched on, however, the Germans became less

14

pleasant and we all had to be very careful in everything we said and did.

I remember how amused we all were when the Germans first began to drive on our roads. They kept crashing into each other with their big lorries. They weren't used to our narrow winding roads. Not only that – the States altered all the road signs before the Germans arrived!'

Mrs. Linda Collenette and son, David

A Jersey resident, Mrs A.M. Priddy, recalled her early encounter with a German officer: 'My old restaurant, The Marina Café, was situated just above Portelet Holiday Camp, so when the Germans took over the Camp, I closed. A couple of days later there was a knock at my front door and a little German officer stood there. He asked me what my premises were. I told the officer that it was a restaurant. He asked me if I was open for business but he could see I wasn't because of the chairs stacked in piles and the childrens' toys all over the floor.

'He asked who lived in the building with me and I told him; just me and my two small sons. Then he asked me where my man was. I told him that my husband was somewhere serving with the British Army.

'The officer looked at me for a moment and said, "I advise you to get a permit, or whatever is necessary to open – otherwise I will have to billet German soldiers on you, which will not be nice."

'He was a nice old boy and frequently came into the restaurant for coffee after that.

'Most of the Germans who came in the cafe were very good and I sometimes found a loaf of bread on a chair when I was cleaning up. When the soft fruit was ripe on the trees and bushes, very often one of the soldiers would take one of my boys up to the garden of a house they were occupying so that they could pick some fruit for me.

'I had my restaurant open throughout the Occupation. Customers had to bring rationed goods such as potatoes and bread with them but we supplied the rest – mainly rabbit stew or chicken. We managed to keep our Aga cooker going mainly on conkers, which my young sons collected on the headland.'

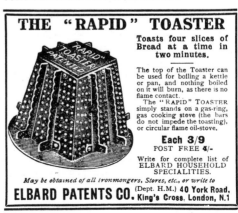

Evidence of the celebrated 'V-sign' campaign. (Copyright: Jersey Evening Post)

Once the Islanders accepted the presence of the German Occupying Forces, it was a case of knuckling under and getting on with life. Their main aim was to find food and income – and cause as much mischief and inconvenience to the Germans as they could.

The Islands were not large enough to support a resistance movement but many civilians risked life and limb carrying out minor acts of sabotage, such as cutting telephone wires, puncturing the tyres of German vehicles, and pouring sand into their fuel tanks.

The celebrated V-sign campaign caused the German authorities a great deal of frustration. As a mark of their continued allegiance to Great Britain, a number of brave Channel Islanders began chalking V-signs on walls, fences, pavements and German vehicles. Two Jersey girls and a Guernseyman received prison sentences of up to one year.

German troops daubed their own brand of graffiti – 'Wir Fahren Gegen England' (We Travel Towards England) – on bunker walls.

An underground newspaper emerged in Guernsey in May, 1942. Known as GUNS (short for, 'Guernsey's Underground News Service'), the paper appeared almost daily for nearly two years and carried valuable items of news culled from BBC broadcasts. Its editors were finally betrayed to the Germans and publication ceased.

For food, Jersey found it comparatively simple to switch from its standard crop of potatoes to grain. Being smaller, Guernsey was less well prepared, and its best glasshouse crops turned out to be sweetcorn. Soya beans were tried but the Island's soil was unsuitable.

The German authorities requisitioned and later commandeered vast supplies of food and main commodities were quickly depleted. Self-raising flour, vinegar, breakfast cereals, baking powder, treacle, vegetable and meat extracts, jam and marmalade and toilet rolls were quickly exhausted. Islanders were forced to seek or create alternatives.

After a time even essential commodities ran out but, encouraged by frequent and helpful advice from the Islands' newspapers, civilians were able to sustain themselves until the end of 1944, when the threat of starvation became a terrible reality.

At the beginning of 1945 the food situation throughout the Channel Islands was so desperate that all communal feeding centres closed down.

The Germans issued orders that anyone found stealing from fields or glasshouses would be shot.

When news of the Islanders' plight reached Winston Churchill, he insisted that the Germans were solely responsible for the food supplies of the countries they occupied.

Troops of Machine Gun Battalion 16 relax on the beach at St. Brelade's Bay, Jersey, during the Spring of 1944. (Photo: K. Spangenburg. Copyright: Channel Islands Occupation Society, Jersey Branch)

THE TURN OF THE SCREW

Several months before the German Occupation of the Channel Islands became a chilling reality – and prior to the 'demilitarization' announcement – the States of Jersey and Guernsey devised a fair food allocation system and issued ration books.

British Ministry of Food directives and advice had been received and published by the Islands' newspapers and Food Minister, Lord Woolton, offered his usual words of comfort and commonsense:

'There is only one line of defence which all of us can hold. It is the line of Food Defence, where we must be constantly on our guard to prevent waste. We must be provident and adaptable. We must seek, day to day, to make the best use of varying food supplies. We must take thought about our food and plan our buying and our cookery wisely.

'Plan your meals. Never use the oven to cook a single dish'

'Whatever happens, you shall have food. When the question is shells or sugar, I know what your answer will be.'

In a BBC broadcast in May, 1940, Lord Woolton announced that the nation's sugar ration was to be cut from twelve to eight ounces on May 27; the butter ration would be reduced from eight to four ounces; and the bacon allocation would be reduced.

The Kitchen Front advised on domestic economy:

'In the kitchen the possibilities for economy are almost limitless. At the moment it is easy to economise on fuel, as cooks are taking full advantage of vegetables and fruit which can be served uncooked. Women are now trying to plan meals that leave nothing on the plates. Simple foods need not be monotonous. Here is a slogan for every woman: "Make less *do* more".'

Newspaper advertisements captured the fervour of the period with slogans like 'Hugons Help Rationing'; 'Oxo – First Aid For The Larder'; 'Royal Arrowroot Dessert – The New Delicious Nourishing Sweet – 'Needs No Sugar'; and 'Sundew Margarine – Quality and Economy Perfectly Combined'.

Britain's Kitchen Front pushed its national message across incessantly: 'It is not only the amount of food that matters. We must eat the right food.'

The prohibition of British newspapers in the Channel Islands soon ended this source of information and solace.

At one time the Channel Islands even considered adopting its own wartime food slogan of 'A Salad a Day Keeps the Doctor Away', but the idea was not pursued, but the population was urged to 'Drink More Milk', and to 'Hatch Every Egg Possible!'

Food manufacturers, Government Departments and national newspapers published hundreds of special wartime cookery books to assist the housewife. A number of these reached the Channel Islands between 1939 and 1940 and, among the most successful and widely available were 'Thrifty War-Time Recipes', published by Good Housekeeping magazine; 'The Stork Wartime Cookery Book'; and Hugon's 'Torox Cube Recipe Book', compiled by popular columnist and cookery author, Helen Burke.

Guernsey's *Star and Gazette* issued a helpful booklet entitled 'Hints On War Time Cookery', which included recipes for Red Pottage, Rabbit Pie, Guernsey Bean Jar and Sweet Corn and Potato Pie.

In his short preface to 'Hints on War Time Cookery', John Leale wrote:
'I have been asked to explain that it is

issued with a dual purpose. Firstly, that of saving fuel, for all the recipes can be cooked in a baker's oven, and it cannot be too strongly emphasised that the more people who avail themselves of this form of communal cooking the longer will our slender supplies of fuel last . . . Secondly, that of helping the housewife to make up attractive dishes during the coming months, when she will have less and less variety of food-stuffs from which to choose.'

This local Channel Island publication, issued by the Controlling Committee of the States of Guernsey, could not have anticipated the nightmare to come.

By December, 1940, the German Authorities had begun to turn the screw. Discipline tightened, rules and regulations multiplied and it soon became very apparent to the Islanders that the velvet gloves had been slipped off and the full might of Nazi tyranny was about to be unleashed on them.

The hoarding of food had already been forbidden by the States of Jersey and Guernsey and by August 10, 1940, all housewives were made to sign a declaration that not more than one month's reserve of food was to be kept in hand. Those with money to spare promptly rushed out to buy every available item of food, depriving many less fortunate of vital supplies.

The Germans delighted in 'lifting' stories from the British press and turning them to their own advantage. One such story concerned the wholesale theft of food-stuffs and was published in the *Guernsey Star* of February 21,1941, under the banner headline: 'Food Robberies Increase In England':

'United Press reports from London that Scotland Yard has issued a statement that the activity of organised bands of thieves is increasing in London. It appears that the continued robberies of foodstuffs are cleverly organised. The

Potato clamps on Occupied Jersey. (Copyright: Jersey Evening Post)

stolen articles are carefully concealed in cellars and re-sold by irregular means.'

Stories of this nature were often completely fabricated and published in a bid to undermine the morale of the Channel Islanders.

Hoarding and theft of food were regular occurrences during the Occupation and were reported in detail by the Islands' press. One daring theft of meat from a butcher's van took place in broad daylight and the thieves actually succeeded in cutting a large hole in the vehicle's roof.

A piano-tuner, accused of stealing 105 tins of 'various commodities', eight pieces of soap and a bottle of lime juice, was sentenced to one year in prison but had his sentence deferred 'on taking an oath of good behaviour for one year.' The prisoner replied to the magistrate, 'I am willing to extend that period for as long as you wish, Sir.'

Fourteen days hard-labour was the sentence meted out to the individual who stole rhubarb valued at two shillings and sixpence. The man also pleaded guilty to stealing several cabbages from the same garden. Two dairy workers were each sentenced to six months' hard labour for stealing milk. A man convicted of stealing 10 pounds of potatoes was

Jersey Evening Post Press Censor at work. (Copyright: Jersey Evening Post)

sentenced to four days in prison. He claimed he was out looking for rabbit food and 'found the potatoes under some bindweed.'

The German Press Censor appeared to delight in publishing stories concerning food hoarding and its penalties. The following report captioned, 'Food Haul In Jersey House', was a superb example of over-the-top journalistic licence and could have only been written by a reporter with a delightful sense of humour. Perhaps it was a sublime attempt at 'getting one over' on the Germans.

'Much excitement was caused in the Town on Saturday by the display in a shop window in King Street, of foodstuffs collected from a residence by the German authorities in the course of a search for food hoards and black market goods.

'There were displayed not only the bacon, but delicacies unseen to the

ordinary eye and untouched by the ordinary tongue for years. The show seemed too overwhelming for some of the surging throng that struggled for a closer view. Strong men reeled at the sight of a group of hams huddled together in naked modesty and shrinking from the bold sparkling gaze of bottles of champagne and brandy.

'Women's eyes grew dim gazing at the packets of tea flaunting their pre-war labels; tinned goods, the sort that had long been dreams of the past, glittered brazenly; fat hugged itself in numerous jars; sugar gleamed whitely at the flour, its neighbour.

'Lashings of eggs nestled in blank, unsmiling smoothness; bacon lay heaped cosily in its tub – but this outpouring is not intended to spin itself to a pre-war Christmas shopping list. Suffice it to say that all the eye has longed for and the stomach groaned for was there.'

The entire hoard came from the home of one man, described by the Jersey Press as 'gluttonous'.

A chilling reminder of the possible severity of punishment for such flagrant breach of the law came at the end of the story: 'Hoarding and black-marketing to such an extent is a crime that does not deserve to be punished by ordinary methods'. It is not known what happened to the culprit.

WEAK STOMACHS AND LIVER COMPLAINTS.

THOMPSON'S

DANDELION COFFEE

1lb. NET.

TRADE MARK

To supplement dwindling stocks of flour, redundant and derelict wind and water mills were put back into action in Jersey and Guernsey. Where possible retired millers were located and returned to work in the refurbished mills.

The Germans attempted to maintain a strict check on how much flour was produced but with limited success. Most attempts at flour control by the Germans met with great resistance from the millers and the enemy was frequently made to look stupid and humiliated. Mill workers often smuggled out small amounts of flour in their socks and boots.

Initially Jersey possessed greater food resources than Guernsey and on at least one occasion sent gifts of potatoes and flour to its neighbour as a gesture of mutual friendship. Guernsey, in turn, sent gifts of fresh tomatoes to Sark.

With its British export outlet for tomatoes cut off, Guernsey, in 1940, saw its entire crop left to rot. A few tons were sent to neighbouring Islands and people did what they could to bottle and preserve as many tomatoes as possible for winter use.

Until the advent of the German Occupation, Guernsey had received food imports amounting to 16,636 tons annually. These imports could not be adequately compensated for and

Guernsey's plight was further aggravated.

The bartering of foodstuffs was strictly forbidden by the State and German authorities but the plucky Islanders managed to over-come this problem in a modest fashion by availing themselves of Exchange & Mart columns in their local newspapers.

Jersey's *Evening Post* of April 28, 1941, for example, featured three columns of small ads, and included the following:

'Pair Gents Wellington Boots (size 9), almost new. Exchange for Foodstuffs and Soap Powder' . . . 'Will exchange Queen Victoria Golden Sovereign for Foodstuffs' . . . 'Wanted Urgently, Golden Syrup and Marmite for excellent offer in cash or any other

consideration if required' . . . 'Exchange quantity of children's clothing, both new and part used, ages 4 to 5 years, for FOODSTUFFS' . . . 'Exchange jar Virol and Brand Beef essence for Household soap and soap Powders', and so on.

As the non-bartering rules began to be implemented, the Islanders merely re-worded their adverts to read, for instance: 'Cycle Dynamo, complete, for best cash offer, or what?' The subtle addition of 'or what?' came to signify foodstuffs.

The tightening of food ration allocations – often out of spite by the Germans – led to the development of a thriving but highly illegal black market within the Channel Islands. There were actually two black markets; local, and relating to butter, milk, eggs and meat, for those who could afford them – and a French black market arising out of maritime trade between the French and Germans. French sailors often brought into the Channel Island ports large quantities of butter, eggs, cheese, cigarettes and saccharine, which were sold to the highest bidder.

According to Dr A.N. Symons, writing about the wartime black market after the liberation of the Channel Islands: 'The unfortunate people were those who lived on retired pay and had few friends, perhaps elderly and not strong enough to stand in queues or walk long distances to find extra food; more especially if they lived alone'.

Other people, of course, benefitted greatly from the circulation of black market goods. In January, 1943, the black market price for a packet of strawberry jelly crystals had risen to ten shillings, while a tin of Bisto retailing in 1939 for ninepence-ha'penny, reached as much as twenty-three shillings. A bar of Black Market Sunlight Soap commanded an even higher price – twenty-eight shillings!

Battered survivor of the Occupation. (Author's collection).

24

Penalties for black marketeering were severe and four Jerseymen appearing at the Military Tribunal of the Field-kommandantur, of St Helier, in 1942, received prison sentences of between five and twelve months for illegally slaughtering and selling the meat from a number of cows and pigs. Heavy fines were also imposed.

A market-stall holder, found guilty of a fourth charge of profiteering, was sentenced by the Royal Court for overcharging on melons to four weeks' hard-labour, a fine of £10, made to refund excess profits and pay £8.10s costs, or serve a further week!

In spite of the rigid laws brought in to prevent black market activity in meat, large numbers of calves and pigs were slaughtered and sold, a good proportion of the meat going to the working man. The working class received extra food by working for the Germans. They offered better wages and more food to attract workers. It was not generosity on the Germans' part but an extension of their overall propaganda campaign.

The first weekly food ration allocated in the Channel Islands had been reasonably generous in the circumstances and included 12 ounces of meat, including fat and bone; 4 ounces of butter; and 4 ounces of sugar.

Bread, milk, potatoes and fish were not rationed at this stage but even then people complained of deprivation.

Meat queue outside Pommier in Fountain Street, St Peter Port, Guernsey, 1941. (Copyright: German Occupation Museum, Guernsey)

Two such raids occurred on August 9 and 11, 1940, when British aircraft attacked Guernsey Airport, killing five German soldiers and wounding four civilians. A similar raid took place in January, 1942, when three RAF Beauforts carried out a low-level attack on St Peter Port, hitting two ships and killing a number of Germans and civilians. The Germans eventually responded to raids of this kind with an official notice, part of which read:

'If in consequence of these raids the RATIONS of the ISLAND POPULATION have now decreased, the population can thank their countrymen ON THE OTHER SIDE OF THE CHANNEL. Churchill and his supporters will not achieve any military success from such nuisance raids.'

Within seven days of these rations being announced the allocation of cooking fat was halved to 2 ounces. A few weeks later 'meatless' days were introduced and the States were forced to issue stern warnings against ration abuse:

'A much stricter watch is to be kept on ration dodgers. Local organisations are to 'put on the screw' to see that rationing regulations are carried out to the letter and as a result many more prosecutions are expected.'

Food ration cuts were ordered by the Germans from time to time as reprisals for the sinking of their ships by British aircraft in the Channel, or for what the Germans dubbed, 'Nuisance Raids' by the British Military Command.

As stocks of essential food supplies grew steadily less, the German authorities reached a mutual agreement with the Island States to import supplies from France. Jersey and Guernsey raised funds from the sale of motor cars – among other things – to Germans, to enable Islanders to purchase meat, flour and medical supplies from French sources.

A joint Channel Islands' Purchasing Committee was formed and headed by Raymond Falla, of Guernsey, and Jerseyman John Joualt. Their operation met with success and during the first week of September 1940, Jersey received its first supplies from France. On October 21, Guernsey received a cargo of 382 tons of supplies from France. These supplies were maintained on a fairly regular basis.

By the summer of 1944, life in the Channel Islands took another downwards plummet when the Allies landed in France and assaulted the Normandy Beaches, cutting off the supply of French food, fuel and medicine. The loss of the Islands' vital French connection also had a profound effect on German supplies. The Germans began to requisition food supplies specially grown for the civilian population. Jersey lost all of its flour to the Germans. It was estimated at that time that all reserves of food in the Channel Islands would be exhausted by the end of November, 1944.

The Germans had placed restrictions on fishing when they first arrived in the Channel Islands and commandeered twenty per cent of each catch for themselves. Although there was an abundant variety of fish available to Channel Islanders from the coastal waters, German regulations concerning

permits, escort of boats, permitted fishing times, rationing allocations – and heavily mined beaches – took their toll of the bounty to be had from the sea. The distribution of fish was, at the best of times during the Occupation, unequal.

Many Islanders openly defied orders and wandered on to restricted beaches in search of cockles, periwinkles, mussels, sand-eels, limpets and ormers. A few men were killed by German mines while hunting for ormers at low tide. Ormers (*Haliotis turberculata*) were held in high

Ormer and limpet shells.

27

esteem by Channel Islanders. Also known as abalone, sea ear, or mutton fish, the ormer was collected from beneath rocks at exceptionally low tides between the end of October and the latter part of April.

Opinions varied as to the culinary merits of this univalve mollusc. A number of sources elevated the ormer to gourmet status, whilst others claimed the shellfish was rubbery and almost inedible. Nevertheless, several ormer recipes were produced during the Occupation.

On March 17, 1941, a 'fair catch of ormers' was reported in the press; up to fifteen dozen of the shellfish being gathered and sold at 4s a dozen in the shell, and £2 for the entire contents of one cross-handle wicker basket. In Sark one fishing boat gathered two thousand ormers in two days.

The humble limpet was also prized for its food value and J. Elliott of Mont Millais, St Helier, sent the author a wartime recipe for Limpet Omelette. Limpet Casserole was another Occupation favourite.

Spider crabs were also highly prized by Channel Islanders and several recipes for the preparation of these crustaceans were featured in the Islands' newspaper cookery column. Mainland fishermen used the spider crab for bait but Channel Islanders considered the flesh of the crab to be superior to that of the lobster.

La Corbiere, Jersey, showing German military construction. The structure has now been erazed. (Copyright: Jersey Evening Post)

CUSTODIANS OF THE LARDER

Local newspapers assisted the Channel Island housewife in every way, advising on how to prepare vegetables in new and exciting ways, which fruit to preserve and encouraging readers to contribute long-forgotten recipes. Labour and fuel-saving hints were regularly published.

Cookery columns were commissioned from a States Domestic Expert. One valued contributer to these columns was Dorothy Pickard Higgs, whose own book, *Life In Guernsey Under The Nazis, 1940-45*, was published in 1947. Dorothy Higgs' cookery notes and recipes, published in the *Star and Evening Press*, made full use of limited food resources and brought into full focus the terrible plight of the civilian population of the Channel Islands.

Both male and female readers of Dorothy Higgs' popular columns were quick to respond with their own recipes and hints and wrinkles.

Britain's Kitchen Front received massive encouragement and official recognition from government departments, BBC wireless programmes, national newspapers and magazines. The nation's 'Dig For Victory' campaign was an enormous success but it should be remembered that neither the effects of it, nor the fervour of Britain's Kitchen Front, were of much benefit to the Channel Islands. The Islands were cut off from all official communication with the mainland and it was left to people like Dorothy Higgs, newspaper editors and a few other individuals to create a Channel Islands' Kitchen Front.

At least one 'Digging For Victory' story was published in the local press before the German Occupation brought an end to such patriotic coverage. The story concerned Mrs J Courharou, of Cobo, who, at the advanced age of 87, still managed to tend her own garden. 'This hardy old patriot has forked her own patch of potatoes and could do the job unaided, too,' claimed the report.

Always something for supper or sandwiches

Libby's

Libby's Corned Beef

KEEPS IN ANY CLIMATE

Pigs in Victoria Street, Alderney, after the island's complete evacuation in 1940. (Copyright: German Occupation Museum, Guernsey)

and fats in the winter time. Also that cattle, animals and poultry have to be fed. Potatoes are our mainstay.'

When the needs of Jersey, Alderney and Sark were also taken into account and added to the final civilian meal tally, which included several thousand slave workers of the Organisation Todt, the States' Committees were faced with a truly frightening prospect. However, they attempted to meet the challenge with great resolve and, in the final stages of the German Occupation, unprecedented heroism.

'What do we face now?' asked the December bulletin. 'We know that stocks of proprietary foods are shrinking rapidly and that housewives are hunting daily for supplies. Fortunately the German Authorities have co-operated with us splendidly and assisted our States Purchasing Commission representatives on their travels in France, gathering meat, cereals, coal, coke, chemicals, seeds and various products

The severity of the civilian population's food dilemma was fully appreciated by the Island authorities. In December, 1940, the States issued a press bulletin under the heading: 'What Rationing Demands of Us Now':

'Our position now calls for serious attention. There is enough food, we believe, for our island (Guernsey) needs, albeit we have to provide for some 92,000 meals per day, or well over half a million meals per week, the year round, with the fact to be faced that the population is most in need of solid foods

Jersey civilians queueing for allocation of meat rationing cards. (Copyright: Jersey Evening Post)

vitally required not only for this year but for the planting out of our fields for the production of cattle food for next year.

'But the outstanding truth to remember in these days is that we, as an island, are drawing week by week nearer to the time when the peace stocks of food and goods are to peter out and we have to face this with a good resolve that whatever privations there may be to bear should be an equal duty on all persons, rich or poor, to observe.

'Let us admit that it is the women who are most worried, since they are the custodians of the larder in each home. It is they who are most painfully aware that the little stocks of reserves are almost gone . . .'

Another writer of that period was Marjorie J. Bird, who compiled a detailed Occupation diary and 'Notes From The Kitchen Front', and whose cookery experience was passed on to relatives, friends and acquaintances.

Communal cooking was one answer to diminishing fuel supplies. Trees were being felled at an alarming rate to provide logs and firewood for Germans as well as locals. The Germans' lumbering horse-drawn field-kitchens consumed vast amounts of fuel. Domestic coal and coke were in desperately short supply and, to make matters worse, household gas was placed

31

on ration from August, 1941.

'Besides the forever worry of food during the Occupation, was the ever-present worry of how to cook it,' Marjorie Bird recalled. 'My original means of cooking was by gas but this was rationed and started at 200 feet per week for two people. Two months later it was increased to 300 feet. My diary states on that day: "We felt extravagant."

'I used to note in my diary what my meter should read each week. If the quarterly reading exceeded the amount allowed, the supply was cut off until the required period had elapsed.

'The supply was only on from 7.30am until 12.30pm, and from 5.00pm until 9.00pm, so household routines had to change. Pre-war vacuum flasks were worth their weight in gold. We used to keep things hot for supper, or for illness during the night. When the flasks inevitably broke, they could not be replaced.'

Communal eating and bakehouse cookery became vital necessities in the Channel Islands during the Occupation and both were extremely well organised by States and public alike. Marjorie Bird remembers bakehouse cooking in detail:

'Every day – and mostly twice a day – my husband, or I, would go down the hill to La Fontaine Bakery, laden with a 14 pound stone jam jar in a bucket, or a baking tin tied up in a cloth. The jar would contain soup of some sort, or much more usually, cut up, mixed vegetables. Potatoes or vegetables would be baked in the tins, with sometimes a basin in the middle containing a pudding, of sorts. There were all kinds of concoctions – some smelled much better than others when cooked!

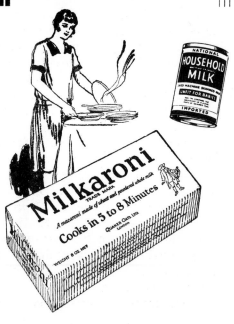

German troops marching past the Town Church, St Peter Port, Guernsey, 1940. (Copyright: German Occupation Museum, Guernsey)

'This bakehouse cooking was done in the hot ovens after the bread had been baked. I believe that most bakehouses carried out this service. The bakehouse was quite a meeting place, an opportunity for news of all kinds to be passed on – out of earshot of the Germans.

'Bakers provided this baking facility for the princely sum of twopence a container – and the baker had to top up the jars with water during the cooking.'

Bakehouse cooking became restricted from September, 1943, when bakers could not cope with the demand, and many housewives revived the art of hay-box cookery and other ingenious methods of preparing hot meals.

In the meantime newspapers, ever

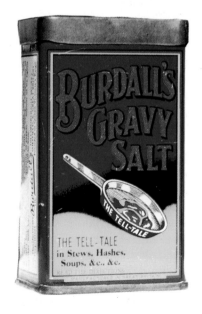

under the watchful eye of the German censor, continued to boost Island morale with homely advice and economy measures.

Jersey and Guernsey restaurants had come into being, inspired no doubt by Winston Churchill's British Restaurants, and 'aimed at catering largely for men whose wives had left the Islands, and who have to do their own housework and cooking.'

The local press ran a brief story about the merits of the restaurants but offered some cynical views regarding the capability of men in the kitchen:

'Many men have sufficient culinary knowledge to enable them to fry bacon and eggs, and, certainly, most men can brew a cup of tea with a savoir faire equal to that of a woman. But we are living in days when frying is out of fashion because of two principal facts (1) the conventional and traditional foods for frying are absent from our larders; and (2) frying is not an economical way of cooking food.'

Soup kitchens also became extremely popular on Jersey and Guernsey. Most were of good quality and offered substantial and nutritious broths made from carrots, potatoes, parsnips, swedes, beans, onions and cauliflowers.

Peter Girard, Headmaster of Occupation Intermediate School and the Castel School, Guernsey, was in charge of the Cobo Children's Soup Kitchen but, he recalls, 'It was not a happy time to be a Headmaster.' Peter and his team of cooks and suppliers coped amazingly well. Between August, 1943, and the end of the Occupation this particular soup kitchen supplied a total of 21,504 meals.

A severe shortage of root vegetables often caused great problems for Peter Girard and his team but the Cobo Soup Kitchen would occasionally receive an unexpected donation from a benefactor. Such a person was Theo Le M. Allez who, as 'Controller' of vegetables, managed to 'divert' ten tons of vegetables from German appropriation to the Cobo soup boilers. When one considers that the penalty at that time for stealing a loaf of bread could be a three-month prison sentence, it will be appreciated what a terrible risk was run by Theo Allez.

At other times local butchers would leave meat attached to bones consigned to the Cobo soup kitchen.

It was not long before bread, potatoes, milk and fish were added to the growing list of rationed food. A minor scandal raged in Jersey over the commercial production of a potato derivative known as potato flour.

Although adequate supplies of potatoes existed in Jersey in the opening months of the Occupation, and enough land existed for their continued cultivation to support the Island's demand, vast quantities were consumed by the Germans – and hundreds of tons were wasted in an effort to produce potato flour on a large scale.

Guernsey had already condemned the production of potato flour as wasteful but the Jersey authorities pressed on regardless.

Potato flour was a centuries-old discovery which re-emerged from time to time and was used to good effect on mainland Britain during the Great War, when the nation embarked on its great allotment drive. The manufacture and use of potato flour was also recommended in countless cookery books published between 1939 and 1945.

It required between thirteen and fourteen pounds of valuable eating potatoes to produce a single pound of flour – and the expenditure of much time and energy. The large scale production of potato flour was simply not worth the

Remains of German field kitchen now on display at Jersey's Island Fortress Occupation Museum.

effort where the Channel Islands were concerned, but the Jersey authorities persisted with its manufacture.

The whole potato flour experiment bordered on farce from beginning to end and the situation was further aggravated when it was discovered that surplus potatoes held in store during 1942 had been badly laid down and were rotten. To make matters worse, the Germans commandeered most of the current crop to export to the Continent.

The States of Jersey, realising its folly, called a halt to potato flour production and then hastily organised what can only be described as an Island-wide 'Potato Census'. By this time it was too late and a potato shortage was imminent.

Eggs had all but vanished from the Islands' larders. In Jersey each parish was expected to supply the Germans with fresh eggs but as each parish's turn

came round to contribute to the Germans' egg fund, the hens would mysteriously stop laying. As soon as the Germans realised what was happening they began to appropriate all the eggs they could find. Inevitably, the Islanders went without.

Before long the people of the Channel Islands were obliged to seek alternatives to eggs, sugar, tea, coffee, cooking fat, fruit, jam, tobacco and other everyday items. They experimented and came up with a wide range of creations, many of them unique to the Channel Islands.

When shortages of essential raw materials made it impossible for Channel Islanders to produce traditional favourites like Wonders, Guernsey Gache, Gache Mêlée, Jersey Cake and Guernsey Crackling, they improvised.

'We found great satisfaction in managing to produce dishes which resembled pre-War ones – however vaguely,' wrote Marjorie Bird. 'As the months and years wore on ingredients changed considerably. Flour became oatmeal or 'bean' and 'potato' flour. Sugar was replaced with sweeteners or sugar beet syrup. Butter was substituted for any kind of fat or oil, or simply omitted altogether.'

Naval Observation Tower (MP 2) at Fort Saumarez, St Peters, Guernsey. (Built on an earlier tower)

Wild flowers such as these soften the landscape - but only feet away lie the remains of German military installations.

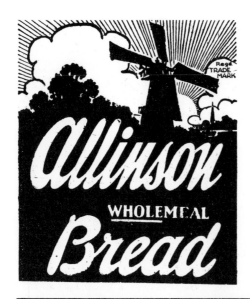

NECESSITY, MOTHER OF INVENTION

The discovery of new food sources and innovative ways with old favourites was no overnight sensation in the Channel Islands. Ever since food rationing was first implemented, Islanders had experimented in the kitchen, but there came a time during the closing months of 1944 when near-starvation drove some people to resort to the sublime and the ridiculous – if not downright dangerous!

Some Occupation dishes and so-called 'cooking-aids' were born out of sheer desperation; others evoked from patient experimentation over a period of months, even years; like the marvellous discovery of sugar beet syrup, and the highly nutritious seaweed called carrageen moss.

A great deal of imagination was employed in the bid to counteract the shortage of flour. Some discoveries, like bean flour, were reasonably palatable – others were little short of health hazards.

Britain's famous wartime 'National Loaf' had no real Channel Island equivalent and the production of good quality bread was fraught with problems. Shortage of white flour resulted in much consternation among Jersey and Guernsey bakers and eventually led to the introduction of wholemeal flour for bread making. In some instances the flour was so 'whole' it contained, among other things, dead insects, string, sawdust, bits of sacking, matchsticks and stones. None of these objects were sifted from the flour and as a result many people who ate the bread baked from this contaminated flour developed a rather uncomfortable tummy upset known locally as 'Jerseyitis'.

Shortage of good quality flour led to other dietary problems and in their

Health & Nutrition report carried out on behalf of the Ministry of Health in September, 1945, Dr Leslie Banks and Dr H. Magee made the following observations:

'The bakers at first made a poor job of baking the high-extract flour; they had little experience of it, and the loaves at first were moist, heavy, and rapidly became mouldy and sour. Gradually they improved their technique and after about three months they were able to produce, especially in Jersey, a really palatable loaf.'

The same could not be said of Guernsey's bread, described by one Island resident at the time as: 'Rather like a cannon ball in weight, tastes sour and gets very stale. I don't think we shall eat excessively of it.'

Guernsey's bread was sometimes maggoty and rancid. It is also worth noting that the grittiness of some of the loaves – caused by the addition of brickdust to the flour – actually caused children's teeth to wear down. To help Guernsey overcome some of its baking problems the Germans even provided one of their own experts who demonstrated the art of making rye bread.

Ship's biscuits, or 'hard-tack', were doled out on more than one occasion to supplement meagre bread and flour rations (around 10 ounces a day for adults). These biscuits were as hard as ceramic tiles and had to be soaked in gravy or water for hours at a time before they could be eaten.

Even prolonged soaking in liquid could not come to the rescue of the cook who mistook plaster of Paris in a tin for white flour and made a pudding which set as hard as a rock in a matter of minutes!

Another resounding flop was the British Bakery Company's 'Tommy Winner' loaf, which came in tins and sold for fourpence half-penny per 2 pound loaf. The 'Tommy Winner' had been advertised in the Channel Islands press in April, 1940, and a glib sales blurb made it sound extremely appetizing:

'Your sample loaf is an excellent type of bread. No-one could take exception to the general appearance of the loaf, which has a natural excellence, and an attractive bright crust colour. We have eaten some when five days old and find it sweet tasting, moist and in good condition.'

Nevertheless, at a meeting of the Master Bakers Association of April 2, it was decided by a majority vote, 'not to recommend the re-introduction of the tinned "Tommy" loaf for sale to the public in the Channel Islands.'

For a time the quality of bread improved and Doctors Banks and Magee noted 'an abatement in the symptoms of diarrhoea.' They further noted that 'constipation, which before the Occupation had been one of the commonest complaints, almost entirely disappeared.'

It should be stressed at this point that the latter condition was also largely attributed to the 'striking effects of change to the increasingly vegetarian diet after the Occupation began.'

Eventually bread became so scarce throughout the Channel Islands that some people resorted to theft. One enterprising felon broke the window of a bakery and stole a number of 2 pound loaves by spearing them on a pole. Another thief broke into a flour stockroom, under the control of the Essential Commodities Committee, and removed one hundredweight of white flour – and promptly left behind a set of large footprints on the dusty floor!

'Gleaning' was another method by

WE'VE GOT TO KEEP WITHIN OUR
FUEL TARGET

which many Channel Islanders supplemented their flour ration. Linda Collenette was among those Islanders who defied the Germans to provide morsels of food for her family.

'As far as the flour was concerned, we used to go gleaning when and wherever possible, collecting wheat. We weren't supposed to do it but it helped to eke out our ration, which wasn't very much. They were dreadful times but we had to make the best of it.

'My husband, Albert, was a Staff-Sergeant in the R.E.M.E and went to France on D-Day. He served in France and Holland. As the wife of a serving soldier I was left here to support myself and my nine-month-old son, David, on 37 shillings a week. It was very hard for us during the Occupation and gleaning was a means to an end.'

Marjorie Bird was another experienced gleaner and in her notes about life during the Occupation, referred to gleaning:

'Crowds of people, mostly women, would wait outside the gates to a field for the farmers to gather up their sheaves of corn, oats, or whatever. Then they would open the gates and we would rush in and gather up any ears left behind. We must have looked like a swarm of locusts. We would then thresh these ears and take the small amount of grain to the mill and exchange them for the same weight in flour. This made a profitable outing for us.'

A recipe for Gleaned Wheat Cake became a great Channel Islands' favourite and was well publicised in the local press.

Frying Pan Scones also found favour.

This Jersey baker found the obvious way around severe petrol restrictions and converted his Bedford van to one horse-power—literally. (Copyright: Jersey Evening Post)

The scones were made from gleaned oats and flour, baking powder and salt and the whole operation took less than ten minutes, from mixing to turning out of greased baking tin – piping hot and ready to eat!

Baking powder could be made in the kitchen from a combination of cream of tartar, bicarbonate of soda and ground rice or cornflour; an alternative raising agent resulted from mixing bicarbonate of soda with vinegar. To hide the flavour of the vinegar a little ginger was used.

When tea and coffee were in short supply Islanders turned to the hedgerows for inspiration.

Bramble tea received good newspaper exposure and one report began as follows:

'Bramble tea, made from blackberry leaves, has become, faute de mieux, a common drink with meals.'

The young leaves of wild strawberries, when dried and brewed in a teapot, produced a decoction similar to China tea. The flavour was further improved by the addition of young bramble shoots and woodruff.

'Tea' was also made from shredded, baked parsnips and carrots, camellia leaves, lemon balm, lime blossoms and green pea pods. The resulting brews were often referred to as 'winklewater'. Bicarbonate of soda was sometimes added to a pot of tea to make the leaves go further.

Mrs A.M. Priddy of St. Ouen, remembers that coffee was made from parsnips:

'Parsnip coffee was simply grated or minced parsnip, dried and roasted in the oven until it became coffee coloured. The parsnips were slightly sweet and made nice coffee.'

Acorns were gathered by local children and sold to shops for coffee making. A

few shops advertised for acorns for this purpose. Dandelion coffee was very popular and, prior to the Occupation, was produced commercially. Perhaps the most bizarre coffee substitute of all was roasted lupin seeds!

A form of grape nuts suitable for a breakfast food or sweetener was produced from grated, roasted sugar beet.

One of the most important Channel Islands discoveries during the Occupation was sugar beet syrup. Producing the syrup was a laborious task and one which Marjorie Bird remembers well:

'Making sugar beet syrup entailed a tremendous amount of work, in washing, cutting up the beet, then cooking it. I did this in a hay-box, mashing it, squeezing out all the liquid, then rendering the liquid down to a syrup. I did this in a basin on a French stove with the rings removed, using cabbage stumps and tar for fuel. It took 20 pounds of sugar beet to make 4 pounds of medium-thickness syrup suitable for cooking, but needing to be thicker – and producing less – for spreading on bread.'

A sugar beet press was later devised, using a spiral car-jack, a strong wooden box and an iron frame.

Sugar beet syrup was commercially produced in Jersey and Guernsey and one manufacturer, N.B. Vaudin of St Saviour's, Guernsey, even had his own labels printed.

Syrup was successfully manufactured from parsnips. Its discovery was attributed to Mrs Saich, who exper-

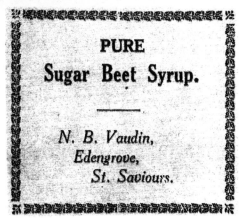

PURE
Sugar Beet Syrup.

N. B. Vaudin,
Edengrove,
St. Saviours.

imented over a period of weeks to produce a perfect recipe.

Parsnip honey was another Occupation innovation and the original hand-written recipe for it is now in possession of the excellent German Occupation Museum at Forest, Guernsey.

Sultanas and currants were produced by cutting sugar beet into small pieces and drying it, or by drying elderberries and locally grown grapes.

On August 12, 1941, the first official notice was taken of carrageen, or Irish Moss, as a food source. It was also used to make cough medicines and hair cream. Carrageen really came into its own as a basis for blancmanges, jams and sauces. Marjorie Bird recalls that carrageen – a frilled seaweed – could be gathered from certain open beaches right up until D-Day but after that the Germans increased Island security and the seaweed could only be gathered with permission from the German authorities.

By that time, however, a number of enterprising chemists in Jersey and Guernsey had produced the seaweed in powder form. One chemist, J.N. Carré, produced Carravita Powder (carrageen blancmange powder) and issued a free booklet entitled *From Seaside To Table,* which contained nine recipes for carrageen.

Ordinary seaweed, or 'vraic' as it was known, supplemented fuel supplies and fertilizer. When burned on an open fire vraic gave off rather acrid fumes and it was only used as a last resort. Vraic was a rich source of fertilizer in the Channel Islands and was once gathered commercially in special two-horse carts fitted with drainage slats.

Toothpaste was another commodity which could no longer be obtained, so chemists ground cuttlefish shells to a fine powder and sold it as tooth cleaner. Some Islanders even used charcoal, or apples, to clean their teeth.

Grated raw potatoes could be mixed with milk and a sweetener – usually sugar beet or parsnips – and baked in the oven as a substitute for rice pudding.

Guernsey housewives made use of apple windfalls and cider to produce traditional Apple Butter. Jersey produced its traditional Black Butter ('Du Nier Beurre') from apples, cider, liquorice, lemons, sugar and allspice.

When cooking fats and oils became scarce many housewives sought refuge in some alarming alternatives, among them white vaseline, liquid paraffin and linseed oil.

A dish known as Occupation Chips was simply chipped potatoes fried in white vaseline. According to Linda Collenette, it was, 'Quite passable if you didn't think about it!'

Liquid paraffin had been used by many cooks in the North of England to make pastry during the Second World War and it certainly found its way into a number of Channel Islands' kitchens during the same period.

The use of linseed oil as a cooking and frying agent was probably perfected by restaurant owner, Frank Stroobant, at the beginning of the Occupation. Stroobant, who was later deported to an internment camp in Germany for alleged 'espionage activities', ran the Home From Home Restaurant in Guernsey in 1941 and, in the absence of suitable cooking fats, experimented with linseed oil. The oil was brought to the boil, using an onion – and later wood blocks – to absorb the fumes, and then used as a frying oil.

In his excellent book, *One Man's War*, Frank Stroobant (a great Guernsey character and raconteur), also mentions creating 'cream' from a concoction of ice-cream powder, soya bean flour, powdered milk and water.

One man was known to have been so desperate for cooking fat that he used sump-oil from his car to cook a meal – and killed himself. Frank Stroobant also claimed to have carried out unsuccessful experiments with motor oil.

When salt ran out the Islanders turned to the sea. Mrs A.M. Priddy, of St Ouen, remembers salt-making:

'We had to make our own salt by boiling down seawater. We had

Frank Stroobant. Prisoner of the Germans.

The 18th century guardhouse at Plémont, Jersey, adapted to mount a twin MG 34 machine-gun. When this photograph was taken during the winter of 1944/45, this must have been the coldest, most wretched sentry post in the entire Channel Islands. (Copyright: Channel Islands Occupation Society—Jersey Branch)

permission from the Germans to go to Portelet Beach to collect seawater, as all the beaches were out of bounds.'

Other Islanders simply boiled vegetables directly in seawater to avoid the laborious process of boiling out the salt. The latter method wasted much-needed fuel.

A dried pea placed in the salt shaker every time it was filled was said to keep the contents dry in damp weather.

A rather odd-ball creation attributed to Jersey's Sun Works was 'Stew-In-A-Bottle', which sold for threepence a pint and contained a mixture of meat and vegetables. The colour and texture of the stew left much to be desired and the scheme was hastily abandoned in favour of a return to a conventional communal kitchen.

In April, 1941, the Jersey Evening Post carried the report of an invention to aid the home production of potato flour. The story ran as follows:

'We have been shown an ingenious home-made mincing machine, which may be clamped to a table and is eminently suitable for the making of potato flour. The idea is that of a St Mary's farmer, and already four of these little machines are in use in the district. The original machine may be seen at our office.'

Toilet paper was another commodity which quickly ran out and one or two enterprising shopkeepers began converting tomato wrapping paper into suitable toilet tissue. Other people reverted to using the old standby – squares of newspaper threaded through string.

Polishes, shoe cream, metal paste and scouring powder were also casualties of war, so Channel Islanders made their own. Time-honoured methods of scouring were revived by using wood-ash or sand. Wood-ash, when dampened, was also used to remove oil and grease stains from clothing and overalls. Metal paste was made from crumbling stones, whiting, soft soap and turpentine. Red brick dust was used to clean copper pots and pans. Plate polish emerged from a combination of yellow soap, rouge, whiting, ammonia and boiling water. Shoe cream was manufactured at home from white wax, beeswax and turps.

The soap ration could be increased by boiling ivy leaves until soft, then adding one packet of soap powder and one tablet of soap. An old-fashioned Channel Island method of producing soap was published in the press and called for the use of furze (gorse) ash:

'When Madame raked out the ashes of the furze to bake her bread, she put

the ashes in the hole beneath the oven, known as the 'Caquère'. When they were cold she put them in a muslin bag – a linsive – and boiled them – and those ashes made the water beautifully soft and 'soap-suddy' for washing.'

Coal could be made to go twice as far by using common washing soda. A good handful of soda was dissolved in a gallon of warm water, thrown over the coal and allowed to dry. The coal was said to burn twice as long. Coaldust mixed with sawdust and pulped paper was formed into bricks, placed at the back of the fire to dry and used as economical fuel.

Another effective method of providing prolonged heat was to fill a paper bag with damp coaldust, place it at

the back of the fire and allow it to burn undisturbed.

Marjorie Bird remembers how difficult it was to economise with fuel:

'There were odd, small, special allowances of coal, coke or 'eggits' during the five years of Occupation but from the Autumn of 1941, coal was reserved for those with open fires as the only means of cooking. All other households had one-hundredweight of logs each month. I can remember that we bought a tar ration from a man delivering by horse and cart. My husband used to dig up cabbages and broccoli stumps – approximately 2,000 at one time – from friends' fields. We dried these and they burned well – but what an awful smell!'

Electric light was also in short supply and Marjorie Bird remembers how she and her husband overcame that particular problem:

'Electricity was rationed from May,

1942. This was half of one's 1939 consumption but it soon went down to 4 $\frac{1}{2}$ units per week – and then on to just 1 $\frac{1}{2}$ units! This was for two people in a household. From November, 1944, electricity was only on from 6.00 pm until 11.00 pm and then later to 10.30 pm. February, 1945 was the last day of electric light. We improvised with a car head-lamp on a stand, connected to a car battery in a box at the base.'

A novel source of light was cobbled out of an empty Brasso tin, drilled through the lid, fitted with a wick and packed with oil-saturated rags or cotton-waste.

When pots and pans wore out and replacements were unobtainable, the black-smith was employed to fashion new ones from old tins. Linda Collenette still possesses such a pot, made from an empty Klim milk tin:

'Everyday items like saucepans were in short supply. In fact, you couldn't get them anymore. We used to use those bolt on patches at first but when the pots got so bad they couldn't be repaired at all, we used old tins we'd saved. We'd take an empty milk tin to the local blacksmith and he would make a saucepan of it – complete with lid and handle. I've still got mine. It was many years before I realised that the word 'Klim', was 'milk' spelled backwards!'

Several months prior to the German Occupation of the Channel Islands, local newspapers urged the public to aid the war effort by handing in their old biscuit tins. The sum of one shilling was paid for large tins; twopence for smaller ones. Those Islanders who did not sell their biscuit tins had cause to be grateful in the years to come. When gas and electricity supplies were severely reduced, or suspended altogether, the 'biscuit tin oven' emerged and earned official status. Advice on the construction of a 'biscuit tin oven' was published in the press and

read as follows:

'A large square biscuit tin makes a useful small oven which can be used on a trepied or gas ring. Lay the tin on its side and the lid forms a door. A meat grid placed inside will lift the cooking away from direct heat. It only takes a few minutes to heat this oven and a very small flame to keep it hot. A kettle of water placed on top will help to keep in the heat and, incidentally, the water will get hot enough for washing up. If a shelf is put in the middle, several dishes can be baked at the same time. The oven can be used for cakes, puddings, meat, etc.'

A variation of this was the 'sawdust oven', described by Marjorie Bird:

'Some people used a sawdust tin for cooking. A biscuit tin was rammed full of sawdust, which was lit, and smoke escaped from an outlet in the side. The top remained hot enough for a saucepan of food to be cooked.'

Simple cooking could be undertaken in the Jersey Firepot, which saw a revival during the Occupation. *The Evening Post* described the 'firepot' as, 'A handy contrivance made usually from a round paint-pot. It conserves flame and heat so well that a kettle of water can be boiled with a fire of twigs with the same rapidity as when over a gas trivet.'

Hay-box cookery was extremely cheap and effective and enjoyed great popularity throughout the First World War. This method of cooking re-emerged in the Second World War and its use was particularly appreciated throughout the Channel Islands. Marjorie Bird referred to the hay-box in her notes:

'In September, 1943, bakehouses became so restricted for communal cooking that I turned to my hay-box. A

Bottom left: Brasso heater (Courtesy of German Occupation Müseum, Guernsey). Right: The ideal shape and size for a biscuit tin oven. (Author's collection)

50

great big box, approximately 2 feet by 2 1/2 feet, stood next to my gas cooker. It was packed very tight with hay around two large saucepans, with a hay cushion that sat on top of the saucepans under a strong lid. The box was first lined with newspapers. One had to put the saucepans in quickly at boiling point and they continued to cook without further attention. It took much longer, of course, but it was a very effective means of preparing hot food and saved a lot of gas. I also had a small hay-box for a single saucepan.'

Another peculiar method of preparing food in wartime was paper-bag cookery, promoted enthusiastically in 1915 by Ernest Oldmeadow, in his book, *Home Cookery In War-Time*. Paper-bag cookery is known to have been adopted by some Channel Islanders during the Occupation.

In the absence of the correct Soyer bags, as they were called, which contained instructions for paper-bag cookery, Oldmeadow suggested that the cook could 'fall back on the method which good cooks used before we were born.

'Cut a sheet of white paper, of good quality, into the shape of a heart. Place the paper – which you have greased all over – with the point of the heart towards you. Having trimmed and seasoned say, a loin chop, lay it on the right-hand side of the heart. Fold the left-hand side over the chop and twist the edges of the paper together where they meet. Bake the bag and its contents on a grid, in a hot oven, for a quarter of an hour.'

The paper-bag method could be used for steaks, kidneys, liver, fish, game – and sauces.

In the 1940's smoking was not considered the anti-social habit it is today and cigarettes and tobacco were looked upon as essential commodities.

When rations were reduced or exhausted, Channel Island smokers either cultivated their own tobacco leaf, mixed it with vine leaves, or turned to a motley array of substitutes. Among the most popular alternatives to tobacco were dried cherry leaves, coltsfoot, rose petals, dock leaves, clover, sweet chestnut leaves, sweet scented burr and lettuce leaves, which saw a brief return to favour as a 'herbal' cigarette in the early 1970's.

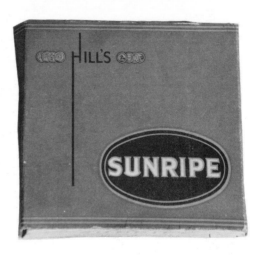

51

Germans and civilians go about their business. High Street, St. Peter Port, Guernsey, 1940.
(Copyright: German Occupation Museum, Guernsey)

German armoured turret bunker, Rocquaine Road, St Peters, Guernsey.

THE CUPBOARDS WERE BARE

A number of Islanders were employed by the Germans during the Occupation. Rates of pay were said to be good by comparison with normal Island wages, and carpenters, electricians and bricklayers were recruited to assist the Germans' building programme. Cooks were also hired to help cater for German troops and slave workers of the Organisation Todt.

The function of Organisation Todt, founded by Dr Fritz Todt, was akin to that of Britain's Royal Engineers, except that OT made use of forced labour and slavery. The total workforce of the Organisation Todt amounted to thousands across the Channel Islands and its demand on the Islands' limited food resources was immense. The workforce was made up of many nationalities, including French, Algerian, Dutch, Polish and Russian. In Jersey a number of Russian slave workers managed to break out of their camp to steal food and clothing.

Food rationing fluctuated dramatically throughout the Occupation but never more so than during the period immediately following the D-Day landings, when it became apparent that Germany had lost the war.

People were forced to adapt to a vegetarian diet of roots and bread and even these commodities were in short supply. According to the medical report of Dr A.N. Symons, 'most of the people, other than farmers, were getting about half their requirements.'

By November, 1944, even the Germans themselves were suffering from lack of food. The Islands' OT slave workers were rapidly approaching the first stages of malnutrition.

Those Islanders who kept goats fared

Le Riche's Stores, High Street, St Peter Port, Guernsey in 1944, when nearly empty. (Copyright: German Occupation Museum, Guernsey)

a little better as the animals provided them with milk, cheese and meat. Goat products were not rationed. A few wily Islanders managed to sneak unregistered pigs through the bureaucratic net and slaughter them for extra meat and bacon rations.

In a poignant scrapbook diary, an anonymous civilian in 1944 expressed the anguish of the Channel Islanders when he, or she, wrote: 'The weather is bitterly cold. We have very little fire and not much to eat. We are now without gas and what a job it is to cook with only one hundredweight of wood a month – and that is all gone. Who would have thought that Dad, at his age, and myself would have to go gathering sticks to make a little fire.'

Ruth J. Ogier in her *Poems on the*

German Occupation of the Channel Islands, captured the essence of the Occupation in a four-line poem entitled, 'Give Me Civilization':

Give me Civilization,
Not an Hitlerised Nation,
Which means Ruination,
And ends in Starvation.

But, as Linda Collenette observed, 'It was the Germans who seemed to suffer most in the end. Not the officers, who were well catered for, but the ordinary men. We almost felt sorry for them at times. It wasn't easy to live with them in our midst without getting to know some of their faces. The slave workers were badly treated, too. A Dutch slave labourer knocked at my door one day, begging for food. I had nothing to give him. My cupboard was bare. There was nothing in it.'

Soon the local newspapers began publishing more and more advertisements for lost cats and dogs. The horrifying truth later emerged that Germans were actually stealing the animals for food.

1930's Peugeot truck, commandeered in France by Germans and taken to Jersey during the Occupation for use as store's vehicle.

The Guernsey Press gave credibility to the 'household pets for human consumption' claim by publishing a story under the heading, 'A Gruesome Theory':

'It has been reported that a gentleman looking for his dog has made the somewhat gruesome discovery of his pet's head and skin. It is inferred by him that the remainder may have found its way into a stew pot! For a considerable time, missing pets have been advertised for in the newspapers, and although there is a great demand for dogs as pets at the present time, all these lost animals have not apparently found new owners.'

The Germans began openly scavenging for food, foraging through the dustbins and stealing from gardens and bakehouses. Six Germans died from eating hemlock, which they mistook for a garden herb. Groups of Germans were seen eating raw swedes; some even resorted to snaring sparrows and pigeons for food; or digging up empty vegetable plots in the hope of finding edible roots.

A handful of civilians, in spite of their own chronic food shortage, still managed to donate a portion of their rations to assist prisoners-of-war, most of whom were airmen.

On November 11, 1944, the Bailiffs of Jersey and Guernsey announced that they had been granted permission by the German authorities to radio for immediate assistance from the International Red Cross. By a cruel twist of fate the Germans, at the same time, ordered a reduction in potato rations to 5 pounds per head, per week.

Eleven days later the German authorities informed the civilian population of the Channel Islands that the International Red Cross had responded to the Bailiffs' plea with a promise of medical supplies, soap and prisoner-of-war food parcels. Furthermore, the Germans pledged not to intercept or interfere with Red Cross supplies when they reached the Islands. Despite their own extreme deprivation the Germans were to honour their pledge.

The promise of assistance from the Red Cross raised the flagging morale of the Channel Islanders but the weeks between receipt of the message and the arrival of assistance were fraught with despair and anxiety. What food reserves did exist were further reduced and it became a bitter fight for survival for the Islanders *and* their German captors.

Artillery Observation Post at La Corbiere, Forest Guernsey, with Observation Tower (M5) at La Provote, in background.

Linda Collenette's saucepan manufactured from a Red Cross Klim milk tin by the local blacksmith.

A basketful of luxuries.

GOD BLESS THE RED CROSS

On December 8, 1944, the Bailiffs received notice that a Red Cross ship was bound for the Channel Islands and was expected to dock in Guernsey during the last week of December. Hopes ran high throughout the Channel Islands and in a diary entry for that period an unknown Islander wrote:

'. . . the Bailiff was informed that our Red Cross boat had left Lisbon and would be here soon. As the weather was rough we thought she would come in on the Monday or Tuesday, but the days went by and she did not arrive. Then the next week we heard she had left for sure again and would be here on Christmas Day or Boxing Day. They also went by and no sign of the boat yet.'

The health of many civilians began to deteriorate rapidly. Most people lost weight and one man lost as much as nine stone.

The gas supply had finished completely on December 21, 1944 and was not restored until June 15,1945.

'We grated raw potatoes and fried the peel,' Marjorie Bird recalled. 'The potato peel was far more appetizing than eating potatoes in their skins. We had to queue for even the smallest amount of food. Often a large swede would be cut in half and sold to two people. We kept rabbits to eat but it became very difficult to find food for them to eat.'

A small percentage of Channel Islanders kept rabbits but the rabbit was probably more useful in providing gravy stock or flavour than as an important source of food.

The anonymous Occupation diary scrapbook, now in possession of Guernsey's La Vallette Underground Military Museum, contained a detailed and moving account of the anticipated arrival of the Red Cross ship. On Wednesday, December 27, the entry read as follows:

Occupation relic.
(Author's collection)

'A great day for all of us – at last our Red Cross Ship has arrived. We have been waiting for her for nearly a month. We had just begun to wonder if she would come, when on December 27, at about 10 o'clock, we heard she had been sighted off St Martin's Point, and that it was true this time.

'At about 2.30pm I went as far as the Platte Mignot and saw her steaming towards the Castle, but she had to wait outside on account of the tide. She finally berthed at the London Berth about a quarter to six. As she came into pool cheer upon cheer went up. All eyes turned towards her . . . she is the Swedish boat, *Vega*.

The International Red Cross steamship *Vega* was built in Gothenburg, Sweden in 1913. With a gross weight of 1,073 tons and powered by triple-expansion steam engines, the *Vega* was capable of a speed of 10 knots. She was owned by Stockholm's Rederiaktibolag SⅤEA and was chartered by the International Red Cross on March 3, 1941. She carried Red Cross supplies and prisoner-of-war parcels from Lisbon to Marseilles and, later, to the Channel Islands.

The arrival of the *ss Vega* had a profound effect on the Channel Islanders and the anonymous diarist wrote:

'Nearly everyone has been as far as the weighbridge to have a peep at our Red Cross Ship, *Vega*. She has a big 'S' on the funnel and across her bows in large letters is written 'C International', and she has many red crosses painted on her.

S.S. Vega leaves Lisbon Harbour, Portugal, March 31, 1945, on its fourth voyage to the Channel Islands. (Photo: Colonel Edouard F. Iselin, International Red Cross. Copyright: German Occupation Museum, Guernsey)

Selection of items from Canadian Prisoner of War food parcel. (Author's collection)

'We thank God for her arrival and for those of the Red Cross who have come to our aid. Our first real contact with the outside world since four-and-a-half years under Occupation. This afternoon at about 1 o'clock they began to unload her.'

On Friday, December 29, 1944, the diary entry read:

'All day today they have been busy unloading the *Vega*. We have to thank the St John's Ambulance and their helpers for the great work they have done for us. They have worked like Trojans so that we can have our parcels for New Year's Day. God Bless You all - though I am sure you were well rewarded when you saw all the smiling faces.'

On her first visit to the Channel Islands the *Vega* carried 750 tons of stores, including over 100,000 prisoner-of-war food parcels, 4,700 invalid diet parcels, soap, salt and medical supplies. The *Vega* made six trips in all to the Channel Islands carrying a total of 460,000 food parcels, most of them donated by Canada and New Zealand. According to one source,

January 3, 1945. Unloading food parcels at St Helier Harbour, Jersey. (Photo: Colonel Edouard F. Iselin. Copyright: German Occupation Museum, Guernsey)

Below: Souvenirs of the Occupation. (Courtesy: La Valette Underground Military Museum, Guernsey)

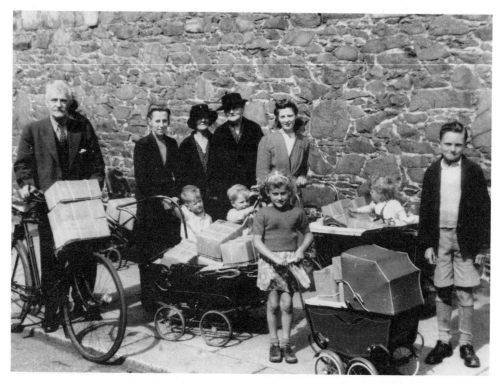

People of Jersey collecting their first Red Cross food parcels in 1945. (Copyright: Jersey Evening Post)

the Islanders 'opened them like children opening presents.' Men, women and children gazed in awe at the parcels' contents – real tea and coffee, tinned meat, chocolate biscuits, jam and fish.

It was not until her third trip that the *Vega* was able to bring flour and yeast for making bread but, in the meantime, the Islanders were able to feast themselves on a dazzling array of luxuries unheard of for five long years.

The food parcels contained the following items:

CANADIAN

6oz tea
2oz biscuits
19oz corned mutton
5oz sardines

15oz lamb and green peas
2oz mild powder
8oz chocolate
6oz prunes
20oz butter
10oz salmon
15oz coffee and milk
14oz corned beef
10oz sugar
8oz raisins
9oz peas
6oz chocolate

NEW ZEALAND

8oz sugar
16oz jam
4oz tea
16oz condensed milk
4oz cheese
15oz cheese
16oz marmalade
6oz raisins
20oz butter
13oz soap
1oz pepper/salt

The parcels were intended to provide each person with 462 calories a day for a month. The Red Cross bread, which came later and amounted to 5 pounds a week – and 6 ounces of flour – gave an average of 987 calories each day.

It would be almost impossible to describe the euphoria created by the delivery of the Red Cross parcels but some indication of the Islands' gratitude may be gained from numerous entries in the aforementioned anonymous diary-cum-scrapbook. This priceless document is filled from beginning to end with labels cut from tins, packets and cartons; alongside each label are poignant observations and general comments relating to the *Vega* and its numerous visits to the Channel Islands. This unknown person spoke for the entire population of the Channel Islands:

'The great day has arrived. We are allowed to fetch our parcels home. It's a long time since the town has seen so many people. Since 9 o'clock this morning people have been busy fetching their parcels – all looking cheerful. They carted them home on their backs, others in carts, prams, bikes, baskets, sacks and vans.

'I am sure that if you could have seen the smiles and cheerful people you

January 3, 1945, Jersey. Front row, left to right: the Captain of S.S Vega, Colonel Edouard F. Iselin, Colonel Heine. (Photo: Colonel Iselin. Copyright: German Occupation Museum, Guernsey)

would have been well rewarded. So, we finished up the 'Old Year' and started the 'New Year' well with great hopes that we will be released. On Sunday the parcels we had given to us were Canadian. My word they were good. Thank you, Canada! for the pleasure you have brought us in these Islands, and the relief which has come to us in our distress, as most of us badly needed them.

'The biscuits were lovely. We soaked and fried some, and some we made into a sup. Our milk powder is called 'Cow Bell'. We hear we are going to have another parcel in about a fortnight's time – a New Zealand one.'

Linda Collenette's Occupation Identity Card and selection of relics from food parcels. (Courtesy: La Valette Underground Military Museum, Guernsey)

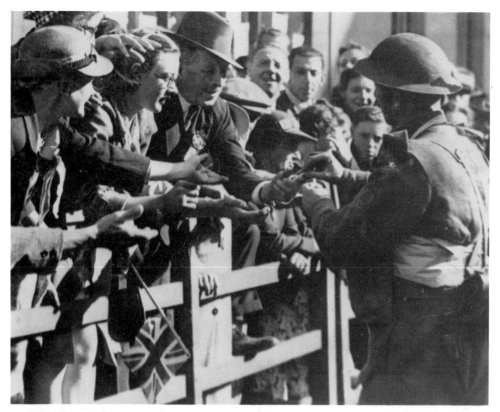

Liberation. A British Tommy hands out welcome cigarettes in Jersey, May, 1945. (Copyright: Jersey Evening Post)

The frustration and anger among the starving Germans at handling the Red Cross parcels for distribution to the Islanders – but having none for themselves – must have been overwhelming. However discipline among their ranks was such that very few parcels were stolen or misappropriated.

One or two Islanders capitalised on their good fortune and sold items from their parcels but those individuals caught by the authorities were dealt with severely, regardless of age.

The war in Europe was over and Hitler was dead but for the Channel Islanders freedom from Nazi captivity was still months away.

When Liberation finally came on May 9, 1945, the Channel Islands had spent five years under Occupation by Nazi Germany. In spite of deprivation, often bordering on starvation, the Channel Islands steadfastly refused to yield to Nazi terrorism. Theirs was a silent battle, waged with fortitude, heroism and perhaps, above all else, the resolve to remain a British people to the bitter end.

The timely intervention of the International Red Cross saved the Channel Islands from a terrible fate. It is sad to reflect that the little steamship, *Vega*, after so many valiant trips to Jersey and Guernsey, was finally broken up for scrap in Stockholm in 1954. If ever a ship deserved to be enshrined as a permanent memorial to the Red Cross, it was the *Vega*.

Guernsey children re-enacting evacuation at a recent Liberation Day Celebration.

The Channel Islands are Liberated. Germans leaving Jersey as prisoners. (Copyright: Jersey Evening Post)

SAME ROOTS, DIFFERENT FRUITS

On April 28, 1945, Dr A.N. Symons, Medical Services Officer, wrote:

'It is known that where there has been severe shortage the decline in health of the population is gradual until the end which eventually comes suddenly. It has been compared to a vehicle going down an inclined plain and then suddenly over a precipice.'

Were it not for the untiring efforts of the Channel Islands' Kitchen Front, it is quite possible that the civilian population might have succumbed before the arrival of the freighter, *Vega*, and her cargo of food parcels.

At the end of the Occupation it was noted that the food situation was actually worse for the Germans than for the civilians. A number of Germans suffered from malnutrition and anaemia and several were emaciated.

The following recipes have been selected from many created by a beleaguered population during five years of almost unbelievable hardship. Most of these wartime recipes can be made today. Most are highly nutritious and cheap to make.

BEAN AND POTATO CAKE

Simply make rissoles from equal quantities of mashed beans and mashed potatoes and fry them in very little fat.

POTATO TART

INGREDIENTS

Potato pastry
potatoes
sugar
spice

Make some potato pastry and roll it out into two rounds. Cover one round with slices of raw potato the size of a five shilling piece. Over each layer sprinkle a little sugar and cinnamon or other spice. Cover with the other round of pastry and pinch the sides well   together. Bake slowly for an hour, take off the top and put in a few spoonfuls of custard or white sauce (cream in other days). Leave till cold and heat it up again when required.

POTATO PUDDING

INGREDIENTS

1lb potatoes
1oz sugar
1 or 2oz fruit
1 egg

Scrub the potatoes, but do not peel them. Beat the egg in a large basin and into this grate finely the unpeeled potatoes, mixing frequently with the egg to prevent the potato becoming discoloured. Add the sugar and fruit and put in a well-greased pie-dish. Bake in a fairly hot oven for about one hour; or the pudding may be steamed for two hours. The fruit may be omitted and the pudding served with stewed fruit or a sweet sauce.

POTATO PEEL CAKE

INGREDIENTS

Several potatoes
4 – 5 tablespoons of flour
sugar or sweetener to taste
1 teaspoon bicarbonate of soda
or baking powder
a little milk
pinch of salt
flavouring if required.

Scrub the potatoes and then peel them. Boil the peels only till soft, drain and mash or mince. Mix the flour with the peel and sweeten to taste. Add the bicarbonate of soda and salt and mix the whole with a little milk and flavour. Bake as for a cake. If preferred, instead of sugar, put onions and herbs and make a savory cake. A few slices of tomato

will improve the flavour. It can be boiled or steamed instead of baked.

POTATO SANDWICH

INGREDIENTS

³/4–1lb of potatoes
1oz of butter
2oz of sugar
1 egg
a little milk

Cream the egg yolk, butter and sugar. Add the cooked potatoes, whipped to a cream with the milk. Add the white of egg and beat to a froth. Put into two greased sandwich tins and bake for half an hour.

SWEET CORN AND POTATO PIE

INGREDIENTS

1lb potatoes
1 small tin sweet corn
1 onion
$1/2$ cup milk
2 tablespoons stale breadcrumbs
$1/4$oz margarine
flour
salt and pepper.

Peel the potatoes thinly and cut them into slices. Half fill a pie-dish with them. Next put in the contents (drained) of a tin of sweet corn and cover with the onion cut into thin slices. Put another layer of sliced potatoes on top, dredge with flour and sprinkle with salt and pepper. Pour in the milk and cover the dish with the breadcrumbs. Dot with margarine and bake for 2 hours.

SWEET CORN PUDDING

Simply mince sweet corn, put it into a pie dish, cover with milk, add sweetener to taste and bake in the oven till done.

COUNTRY BATTER PIE

Braise some chopped vegetables (whatever available) in a little pork fat till tender. Put into a hot, greased pie-dish with slices of cooked sausage or other meat. Pour some batter over and bake in a hot oven for about half an hour.

Agricultural machinery of this type was often driven by steam traction engines. This particular machine saw service in Guernsey throughout the Occupation.

BATTER IN TOMATO SAUCE

Chop the remains of a Batter Pie. Make a white sauce and add a little tomato purée, a pinch of soda and the chopped batter. Serve in a hot dish with a little chopped parsley sprinkled over.

TOMATO BREAD SPREAD

'Many of us regret that we are unable to use as many tomatoes as we would like, owing, as working class people, to not being able to stock sugar and salt. When my wife was here we always had tomato chutney and tomato sauce made each season. Before giving you a useful recipe, I wish to state that I have given some of the undermentioned to several of my friends to sample and they liked it. Before the war I had this spread on bread and butter but under war conditions this will be quite good on bread alone, having margarine included.'

INGREDIENTS
$^1/_2$ *lb tomatoes*
1oz margarine
1oz grated cheese
1 egg
salt and pepper

Skin and pulp the tomatoes, add the margarine and cook for a few minutes. Add the cheese, seasoning and the beaten egg. Stir gently but do not boil. When thick, pour into small jars and cover when cold.

'I generally allow the pulp of an extra tomato to allow for any hard centres in the $^1/_2$ pound, which it is advisable to extract when pulping.'

TOMATO PIE

INGREDIENTS

Tomatoes
butter
1 onion
seasoning
breadcrumbs

Butter a baking dish and cover the bottom with sliced tomato, dot with butter and season. Onto this place a layer of fried onions. Repeat these layers until the dish is full, finishing with breadcrumbs. Bake for 20 minutes in a moderate oven.

TOMATO JAM

INGREDIENTS

To every 1 ^{1}/₂lbs of not too ripe tomatoes, add
^{1}/₂lb sugar
^{1}/₄oz Carrageen
1 cup water

Pour boiling water over the tomatoes and leave for a few minutes. Then peel and slice the fruit and place in a saucepan with a cup of cold water, add a tablespoonful of sugar and the carrageen (previously soaked) and boil for 15 minutes. The jam is then ready to be placed in jars.

CARROT PUDDING

INGREDIENTS

3oz breadcrumbs
1oz sugar
1oz margarine
1 gill milk
2 eggs
2 medium carrots
1 teaspoon ground ginger

Put the breadcrumbs, butter and sugar into a basin and pour the boiling milk over them. Clean and grate the carrots and add them, together with egg yolks and ginger, to the soaked breadcrumbs. Stir in the stiffly beaten whites of egg and bake in a moderate oven till firm and well browned. Serve with custard or ginger sauce.

71

Queueing for buttermilk at Grove Farm Dairy, Guernsey, 1942. (Copyright: German Occupation Museum, Guernsey)

PARSNIP PUDDING

INGREDIENTS

*Cooked, cold parsnip
cocoa substitute
bicarbonate of soda
$^{1}/_{2}$ pint warm milk
sugar or sweetener*

Mix all the ingredients together and place in a greased pie-dish. Bake for $^{1}/_{2}$ hour.

BREAD AND CHEESE CUSTARD

INGREDIENTS

*Bread and butter (left from tea)
1 cupful grated cheese
1 pint milk
2 eggs
pepper and salt*

Grease a pie-dish, cover the bottom with bread and butter, cover with grated cheese, then bread and butter again and more cheese. The last layer should have butter on top. Beat the eggs, add the milk, salt and pepper. Pour into the dish and leave to soak for $^{1}/_{2}$ hour. Cover with grated cheese and bake in a moderate oven for about $^{1}/_{2}$ hour and serve hot.

DAMPER

(This recipe was published in the press following several queries from readers as to its origin. The paper replied: 'As we remember it, it is a sort of bread made by bushmen in Australia, is quickly made and is very palatable.' Damper was apparently eaten in the Channel Islands at the turn of the century and revived during the Occupation.)

INGREDIENTS

*$^{1}/_{2}$ self-raising flour
large pinch salt
enough water to mix a dry
 dough*

Put the dough into a greased tin and put the lid on. Put the tin in a hole in the middle of the fire and rake the fire over it until the tin is covered. Leave for about 15 minutes, remove and eat hot.

LIMPET OMELETTE

INGREDIENTS

2 quarts limpets
1 bay leaf
2 small leaks
1 egg
parsley
salt and pepper

Put the limpets into cold water, bring to the boil, strain and remove shells. Return limpets to the pan and simmer with the bay leaf and a little pepper and salt until quite tender. Strain. Remove the heads and strings and mince the limpets. Chop the leeks and mix them with the limpets, adding parsley. Put a little fat into a frying pan, add the well-beaten egg and then add the limpet and leek mixture and fry till brown.

STEWED ORMERS

(Courtesy of Rocquaine Live Shellfish Ponds, Guernsey)
Soak the ormers in salt water for $^1/_2$ hour, then scrub them with a hard bristle brush. Put into clean water and wash until white. Take them out and beat them with a wooden rolling pin on a wooden chopping board until they become tender, but take care not to break them. Then brown the ormers in a frying pan with butter. They will then look like steak. Next put them in a stew pan with a large onion cut up, season with herbs to taste and cover with a thick gravy stock for 8 hours. They should be as tender as

veal cutlets but far more delicious!

CARRAGEEN RELISH

Boil apples or other available fruit and sweeten to taste. Cook carrageen as usual with milk and flavouring; mix all together and allow to set like a mould.

73

Civilians turn out to watch German prisoners leaving Jersey. (Copyright: Jersey Evening Post)

TURNIP JAM

INGREDIENTS

$1\frac{1}{2}$lbs turnips
$1\frac{1}{2}$ pints of water
1 teaspoon flavoured carageen
(Carre's Powdered Carravita)
1 cupful of raspberry cordial

Boil the turnips until tender, then mince them. Put back into water, add the raspberry cordial and carrageen and boil for 5 minutes. Allow to cool and pour into jars and cover.

Parsnips could also be made into jam, using orange juice as an alternative flavouring.

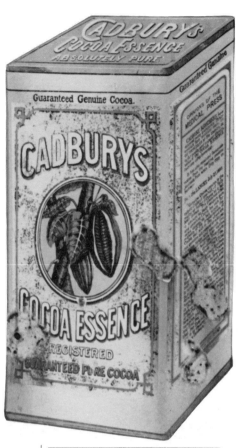

GUERNSEY BEAN JAR/JERSEY BEAN CROCK

This was said to have been the inspiration behind baked beans, the traditional Channel Islands' bean jar, or crock, is a centuries-old recipe which has many variations. In Jersey the Bean Crock was served as a supper dish, while in Guernsey the locals preferred to eat their Bean Jar for breakfast. In spite of food restrictions both Islands managed to preserve rudiments of the Bean Jar/Crock throughout the Occupation.

Put a nice meaty bone in a casserole with a few onions, carrots, a turnip and a pint of beans.Cover with plenty of water and season well. A teaspoonful of treacle and half a teaspoonful of mustard may be added. Almost any meat or vegetables will do and to save gas a layer of potatoes can be put over the top.

FISH PUDDING

INGREDIENTS

8oz pilchard or salmon
1 egg
1/3 pint breadcrumbs
1 gill milk
1 tablespoonful melted dripping
salt and pepper
tomato sauce

Flake the fish with two forks, add the breadcrumbs, seasoning, beaten egg and dripping. Mix to a soft paste with the milk and put into a greased pudding basin. Cover and steam for 1 hour, or until set. For the tomato sauce, boil together a gill of tomato purée and a gill of water. Blend a tablespoonful of flour or cornflour with a little water, pour the tomato over this and return to the pan. Boil for 2 minutes, stirring well, and season. Turn the pudding on to a hot dish, pour the sauce over and serve.

WARTIME YORKSHIRE PUDDING

INGREDIENTS

4oz flour
1/2 pint buttermilk or sour milk
pinch of salt
1/4 teaspoon bicarbonate of soda
(Fresh milk and self-raising flour may be used; is so, omit the soda)

Sift the flour and salt into a basin and stir in the buttermilk. Beat well and stand aside for at least 1/2 hour. Mix the soda with a very little water or fresh milk and stir in just before cooking the batter.

Bake in a hot oven for about $^1/_2$ hour. Cut into sections and serve on a hot dish with a good gravy.

VEGETARIAN SAVOURY SAUSAGE

INGREDIENTS

$^1/_2$ lb haricot beans
6lbs mashed potatoes
$^1/_2$lb onions
$^1/_2$lb tomatoes
2oz margarine
4 teaspoons chopped parsley

Soak and cook the beans; fry the onions and tomatoes in the fat. Pass the beans and other ingredients through the mincer, mix well and add seasoning. Scale at 4oz, roll into sausages, dip in batter and fry a golden brown. These may also be made into balls, rolled in flour and baked in the oven.

BEAN FLOUR

Using scarlet runner beans. Dry the beans in the pod in a slow oven, pass them through a mincer, sift and return to the mincer until the whole has been converted into flour.

BEAN FLOUR CAKE

INGREDIENTS

$^1/_2$lb bean flour
3oz fat
a little milk
1oz sugar
pinch of salt
a few sultanas

Rub the fat into the flour, mix the other ingredients with the milk; mix all together, put into a tin and bake in a moderate oven.

SUBSTITUTE JUNKET

'Consumers of junket may be interested to know that the common wild Lady's Bedstraw (*Galium verum*) which flowers during July and August, is an efficient substitute for calf rennet. In fact, in some parts of the United Kingdom it is named Cheese-Rennet and Curd-Wort. All that is required is to put a sprig of the plant when in flower into a pint of slightly warmed – not hot – milk and allow it to cool.'

BEAN MARZIPAN

Cook some small white beans to a mash. Mince well and leave in a hay box all night. They must be fairly dry. Pound to a smooth paste. Mix in a little sugar and flavour to taste with almond essence. If the beans are too dry, moisten with milk, not cordial, as it will spoil the colour. Baked marrow or squash seeds may be used as substitute almonds for decoration.

HOKEY KOKEY JAM DUMPLINGS

INGREDIENTS

4oz flour
1/4 teaspoon baking powder
2oz margarine
pinch of salt
1oz of breadcrumbs
1 egg
quantity of jam

Make a dough with the above ingredients. Put two or three teaspoonfuls of jam into a saucepan, add a little water, and let it boil. Make dough into small balls and put into saucepan. Put cover on and boil for a few minutes. Turn the dumplings around

and they are ready to serve, using jam left in the saucepan as sauce.

IMITATION SUET PUDDING

INGREDIENTS

8oz flour
small teaspoon salt
4oz raw, peeled potatoes
cold water to mix

Put the flour and salt into a basin, grate the potatoes and mix with the flour and sufficient water to form a soft dough. Put into a greased basin and steam for 2 hours.

PARSNIP HONEY

Peel and wash 3lbs of parsnips. Cut into chunks and cover with cold water. Boil up sharply and simmer until soft. Drain off water but do not throw away. Mash the parsnips. Put liquid back into pan and add the mashed parsnips. Boil slowly and stir for 10 minutes. Pass the contents through a sieve. To each pound of purée add 4oz of sugar; 1 teaspoonful of salt; 1 teaspoonful of ground ginger. Boil all together for 8 minutes. Put into jars whilst hot.

As an alternative to ground ginger, crush a few cloves, tie in a muslin bag and boil with the parsnips. Remove the muslin bag when bottling.

MACARONI CAKE

INGREDIENTS

2oz macaroni, soaked and
 drained
2oz flour
a little butter and milk
baking powder

Mix the flour with the macaroni into the stiff mixture with the other ingredients. Bake for 20 minutes in a hot oven.

Liberated

Also available: the story of Britain's home front effort. Profusely illustrated. £4.95. From bookshops, or direct from Redcliffe Press Ltd, 49 Park Street Bristol BS1 5NT, cash with order.